CONGRATULATIONS!

It appears that they have decided to let you drive despite all of the public safety warnings, and a petition with over 10,000 signatures strongly advising against it.

This book is intended to assist you on your journey to become a safe and responsible driver. At the very least this book should delay you long enough to allow people in your hometown some time to gather up their personal belongings and head for higher ground.

This book will begin with an overview of some VERY basic driving principles that should be very obvious to most people. We have been told that you are not like "most" people. The second and larger portion of the book contains very practical examples of things that you, as a driver, should NEVER crash into. Not even if you think it would look really cool.

These are very important guidelines. Be sure to study these pages thoroughly. One to two years of intense study may be needed before heading out onto the road. There's no rush.

SECTION 1

WHAT IS A CAR AND WHERE DOES IT GO?

AUTOMOBILE (CAR)

Let's start with the basics. This is car. C-A-R.

A car is used to SAFELY transport people and/or objects from one location to another.

This machine is what you will be responsible for controlling. It has four wheels (those round rubbery things at the bottom) that are meant to be in contact with the road at ALL times. Gravity wants that car on the ground. Obey gravity.

Contrary to what video games and movies may have taught you, cars are actually NOT meant to crash into things. In fact, one of the main principles of driving is to avoid coming into contact with other objects and/or living organisms.

Which one of the following four images shows the correct orientation for a car?

Careful!   This one is tricky.

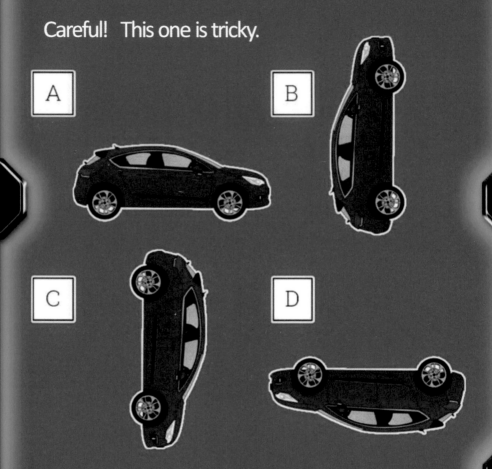

A

B

C

D

The correct answer is A.
If you did not get this correct, please go back and read the previous page several thousand times.

THE ROAD

This is a road. It is a mostly flat surface designed for cars to travel on. This is where your car should be whenever it is not safely parked. The basic idea is that your car should stay on the road between the marked lanes. Interestingly, in North America and Europe, vehicles drive on the right side of the road, whereas in the UK, Japan and Australia, cars drive on the left side.

Important New Driver Information

If you are driving in the USA and speaking with an accent then you are still required to drive on the right side. Your direction of travel does not change with your horrible attempt at an Australian accent.

SECTION 2

THINGS THAT YOU SHOULD NEVER CRASH INTO

PEOPLE

People are everywhere.

There are approximately 7 Billion people on Earth and it is very important that you do not hit any of them. Not even a single one. Let us explain. Cars are made of very hard materials such as metal.

People are essentially squishy meat bags that are not designed for high speed collisions with hard metal objects. Crashing into people can result in vehicular homicide, jail sentences, and is strictly forbidden.

REPEAT (3x):
I WILL NOT CRASH INTO PEOPLE

OTHER CARS

Believe it or not, your car is not the only car on the road, although everyone might be a little safer if it was. Your top secret super mission is to avoid striking, nudging, bumping, grinding or destroying any other vehicles that are on the road. This could be very challenging as there could multiple new drivers on the road at any given time. In scenarios such as this, we just cross our fingers and hope for the best. Some examples of vehicles to be avoided are: cars, trucks, motorcycles, vans, buses, and wayward clown cars.

REPEAT (3x):
I WILL NOT CRASH INTO OTHER CARS

HOUSES

These large buildings are where families gather and live in relative safety from the hazards of new drivers.

Large and strong, these provide significant resistance to cars. While it might seem really cinematic to crash through someone's living room, it is highly discouraged by homeowners and police alike.

REPEAT (3x):
I WILL NOT CRASH INTO HOUSES

09

OLD PEOPLE

Old people are very similar to people in most respects, but are significantly slower.

The elderly are particularly hazardous due to their slow speed. However, please recall that the elderly are extremely sensitive to being struck by large poorly controlled metallic objects. Crashing into old people WILL result in vehicular homicide charges, and is strictly forbidden

REPEAT (3x):
I WILL NOT CRASH INTO OLD PEOPLE

10

PARKED CARS

Parked cars may seem like an inviting target. After all, they are everywhere. Who would even notice if one measly parked car was smashed or rammed into? The owner of the car would, that's who.

Also, your foolishness will be caught by nearby security cameras and at least 100 people on their cell phones. Significant damage would be done to your car as well, which would limit the use of that handy 'Go Places' feature that you like so much.

REPEAT (3x):
I WILL NOT CRASH INTO PARKED CARS

TREES

Little known fact: Trees are hard and made of wood. These two factors place them firmly on the DO NOT CRASH INTO list. You might think that it would be cool if you crashed into a tree and it caused all the leaves to simultaneously fall down. That might look cool, but would also result in you being very dead.

Trees also create oxygen, so what do you have against that? Are you too cool for oxygen?

REPEAT (3x):
I WILL NOT CRASH INTO TREES

PALM TREES

These are similar to regular trees but are generally warmer. These are still highly unacceptable objects to slam into with your vehicle. The impact may result in a volley of coconut projectiles that create panic, chaos, and carnage while attracting swarms food bloggers preaching the benefits of coconut oil.

Use all of your attention and self restraint to avoid these swaying wooden plants of doom. Just enjoy your time at the beach like a normal person.

REPEAT (3x):
I WILL NOT CRASH INTO PALM TREES

13

GARBAGE BINS

Every week, all around the world mystical bins of refuse suddenly appear on street corners like magic. No one knows how. No one knows why. For new drivers, these days are particularly hazardous. Contact with garbage cans, or their distant cousins recycling or compost bins should be avoided. Failing to adhere to these regulations can result in your car being splattered with rotting meatloaf and baby diapers. Don't mess with sanitation workers. They know how to make things disappear.

REPEAT (3x):
I WILL NOT CRASH INTO GARBAGE BINS

ELEPHANTS

Let's say you're driving to the mall and you make a wrong turn. Boom! Suddenly you find yourself in the African savanna surrounded by a herd of elephants. It is imperative that you avoid any and all contact with these magnificent animals.

New drivers are advised to keep a small bag of peanuts in the glove compartment at all times to protect against this situation.

REPEAT (3x):
I WILL NOT CRASH INTO ELEPHANTS

15

MOUNTAINS

Mountains are hard, pointy rocky things that stick up out of the ground. These are not ideal places for a new driver to be. Some mountains may have some roads and tunnels for driving, but to the surprise of many new drivers, not all areas on mountains are accessible by car. Some FAQ

- Can I drive to the top of Mount Everest?
  No.
- What if I start off going really fast?
  Still no.

REPEAT (3x):
I WILL NOT CRASH INTO MOUNTAINS

FENCES

Fences can be made of metal or wood and are very common. Another primary purpose of a fence is to keep reckless newbie drivers from leaving a trail of destruction on private property.

Some fences in high security areas can also be electrified. Some new drivers are literally shocked to learn that peeing on an electric fence is never a good idea. Stay away from fences and they will stay away from you.

REPEAT (3x):
I WILL NOT CRASH INTO FENCES

MAILBOXES

Mail carriers everywhere work very hard to deliver valuable correspondence to your doorstep. Centuries ago (before email, SMS and snaps designed for chatting), people would actually write letters on paper and mail them to each other. Today mailboxes hold valuable things like bills and real estate advertisements, which people everywhere love receiving.

Give mailboxes the clearance they deserve.

REPEAT (3x):
I WILL NOT CRASH INTO MAILBOXES

18

CACTI

If you live in a hot climate, interacting with cacti (a.k.a. cactuses ... cactususes?) could be a part of everyday life. Cacti are basically desert trees that are anti-social jerks. Cacti would prefer to avoid all contact with vehicles if possible so that they can focus on things they really enjoy, like complaining about the heat. "Ughh. It looks like another hot one today."

Accidental contact with a large cactus can result in an explosion of spines, vehicle damage and unwanted high velocity acupuncture treatments.

REPEAT (3x):
I WILL NOT CRASH INTO CACTUSUSES

SAND DUNES

Staying with the hot climate for a minute, we come to the topic of sand dunes. While it is possible to navigate some sand dunes in a vehicle, it generally requires specialized vehicles and local guides who are familiar with the terrain. You should not attempt to cross the Sahara in your beat up 2003 Ford Focus.

More importantly, sand dunes are also notorious for their lack of gas and service stations for picking up snacks.

REPEAT (3x):
I WILL NOT CRASH INTO SAND DUNES

20

FIRE HYDRANTS

We know this is a staple of cartoons and movies. A car skids by, usually during a high speed chase. The car clips the fire hydrant, which cleanly shears off and generates a large vertical plume of water. Dozens of children soon rush in to frolic in the water and beat the relentless summer heat. You're a hero to those kids.

Except that you're not. Your car was destroyed by the giant metal fire hydrant and you are now responsible for $5 million in flood damages. Don't do it.

REPEAT (3x):
I WILL NOT CRASH INTO FIRE HYDRANTS

21

GAS STATIONS

Let's cover some basics. Gasoline (a.k.a. petrol) makes cars go. Gas stations are places to get gasoline. Gasoline is highly flammable.

Most gas station owners prefer to have new drivers fill up their gas tanks at a safe neutral location 15 miles away while under the constant supervision of the fire department. Needless to say, crashing into gas stations is bad, but we'll say it anyway. Crashing into gas stations is bad. Don't. Do. It.

REPEAT (3x):
I WILL NOT CRASH INTO GAS STATIONS

22

THE LEANING TOWER OF PISA

Constructed in the 12th century, the Leaning Tower of Pisa is an iconic landmark in northern Italy. You, being a new driver, unfamiliar with the rules of the road and physics, might mistakenly think that this would be your opportunity to become an Italian hero. Let's get this out in the open. You cannot straighten out the Leaning Tower of Pisa by simply ramming into it at high speed. Italians everywhere will hate you more than ketchup on pasta. Capisce?

REPEAT (3x):
I WILL NOT CRASH INTO THE LEANING TOWER OF PISA

23

BICYCLE RACKS

Remember just a little while ago when you rode a bike and humanity was an order of magnitude safer? You are now swimming in the power of the internal combustion engine. Bicycles now seem childish to you. So silly.

Now a rack full of bicycles looks like a row of bicycle dominoes begging to be knocked over in their ultimate lameness. REMEMBER: Lameness is not a reason to crash into something. If it were, you would have to live in constant fear.

REPEAT (3x):
I WILL NOT CRASH INTO BICYCLE RACKS

24

BIG FOOT

You've done it. You found Big Foot. A Sasquatch! Or maybe even a Yeti.

These are the hide and seek champions of the world, and their streak has come to an end. Maybe you found it in Sasquatchewan, a province in Canada, which seems like a logical place to look. Remember to keep a respectful distance. Give the guy (or gal) a break.

Just take a blurry picture and move on.

REPEAT (3x):
I WILL NOT CRASH INTO BIG FOOT

25

AIRPLANES

Okay this one gets a little complicated, and should go without saying, but let's make sure we have all of our bases covered. First, let's say that crashing into an aircraft is very difficult and not to be condoned. You would have to be travelling at a phenomenal rate (don't do that) and then launch yourself off of a highly inclined ramp (bad idea) to gain enough altitude to cross the flight path of an aircraft (really dumb).

Reminder: Cars can't fly. Well, at least not yet.

REPEAT (3x):
I WILL NOT CRASH INTO AIRPLANES

THE MOON

This one might seem a little out there (pun intended), but is included here for drivers who have their head in the stars. There are several lunar roving vehicles currently sitting on the moon from the Apollo missions so this is not without precedence. Ignoring the logistics of how to get to the moon, you should always remember this handy phrase: Moon up. Earth down. This will help you remember that the moon should never be beneath the wheels of a new driver. The moon has a severe shortage of gasoline and air so this is quite practical advice.

REPEAT (3x):
I WILL NOT CRASH INTO THE MOON

27

SUBMARINES

Most people don't need specific instructions on why it is important to not hit a submarine with your car.... For one, submarines travel underwater at significant depth. Let's assume that this is still well within your range of capabilities.

If you are ever suddenly launched into the mid Atlantic in your car and see a submarine approaching, please do your best not hit it. Just imagine their confused faces as they see a car slowly drift by on their sonar. Captain? You're not going to believe this.

REPEAT (3x):
I WILL NOT CRASH INTO SUBMARINES

28

ICEBERGS

Iceberg straight ahead! If you find yourself saying this you may have been following an uncalibrated GPS for far too long. Icebergs are chunks of ice that have broken away from an ice shelf in the hopes of avoiding questionable drivers such as you. Crashing into an iceberg takes great amounts of luck and stupidity. They are large, hard, cold, wet, unstable and dangerous. You probably have a few things in common. Keep your wheels firmly on the road and away from unstable, jagged floating mountains of ice.

REPEAT (3x):
I WILL NOT CRASH INTO ICEBERGS

ANTARCTICA

Antarctica is home to millions of cute, hardy and peaceful penguins. According to the Antarctic Penguin Health and Safety Organization (APHSO), there were zero vehicle related penguin deaths on the Antarctic continent last year. The same is also true for the preceding million years.

They've got quite a streak going. Let's keep it that way. Keep your car very far away from Antarctica.

REPEAT (3x):
I WILL NOT CRASH INTO ANTARCTICA

30

SNOW PLOWS

If you live in a colder climate then you probably have had to deal with snow plows from time to time. The problem here is that snow plows typically move very slowly, and you, being a newly licensed driver are very important and have places to go.

Give these guys some extra space or you might end up momentarily surfing a wave of snow (Yay!) before crashing into a ditch (Boo!).

REPEAT (3x):
I WILL NOT CRASH INTO SNOW PLOWS

31

CONSTRUCTION EQUIPMENT

Let's summarize it like this.

Construction equipment: Big and strong.

You: Small and puny.

Think of a dump truck, crane, or cement mixer as the heavyweight champion of the world. Now think of yourself as an anxiety ridden gerbil that wets himself when exposed to a gentle breeze. You will not win this fight. Crashing into a construction vehicle will turn your car into a destruction vehicle.

REPEAT (3x): I WILL NOT CRASH INTO CONSTRUCTION EQUIPMENT

SNOWMEN

Snowmen. Snowomen. Snow people.

In today's society we must respect and support snow beings of all kinds. Children or bored teenagers worked very hard to build that snow person. Crashing into it would be a pretty dickish move. If you crash into a snowman, you will be robbing it of its chance to magically come to life one day, which TV has repeatedly shown to be a real and distinct possibility.

REPEAT (3x):
I WILL NOT CRASH INTO SNOW PEOPLE

33

GARDEN GNOMES

It is a generally accepted fact that garden gnomes are creepy. Why are they so happy?

However, much like some people deny that the Earth is round, some people love these creepy little garden demons. While it might seem satisfying to slowly crush these soulless monsters under the might of your powerful wheels, we must remember that the destruction of other people's disturbing possessions is not encouraged.

REPEAT (3x): I WILL NOT CRASH INTO GARDEN GNOMES UNLESS I REALLY HAVE TO

34

LAKES

Lakes are like giant murderous puddles. I'm sure you've seen a truck drive through a big puddle that sends a wall of water in both directions. Maybe they even soaked some poor bystander. Hilarious!

So more water means a bigger splash and more hilarity right? The puddle volume to hilarity equation proves that there is a strong decline in hilarity and exponential increase in sunken cars with substantial puddle volumetric increases.

Stop and think! Lakes make you sink!

REPEAT (3x):
I WILL NOT CRASH INTO LAKES

FARMER'S FIELDS

In front of you lies an endless field of wheat, or corn, or some other valuable crop such as gummy bears. Roads? Who needs roads? Time to drive where no man (aside for generations of farmers) have ever driven before.

Little know factoid: crops are food. They are not just decorative play things to amuse you. Farmers may attempt to harvest you if they catch you messing up their fields

REPEAT (3x):
I WILL NOT CRASH INTO FARMER'S FIELDS

VOLCANOES

Volcanoes are basically mountains with a bad attitude and a drinking problem. Who doesn't want to get irrationally close to a bubbling cauldron of liquid hot magma? And what better way to do it than from the comfortable confines of your air conditioned car?

Fact: lava can melt cars. Lava can melt people. Rubber tires will not allow you to drive on an active lava flow. Leave the stupid lava selfies to dumb Instagram hikers and keep your distance from active volcanoes

REPEAT (3x):
I WILL NOT CRASH INTO VOLCANOES

LAWN MOWERS

Lawn mowers are used to mow the lawn. Cars, trucks, and vans can also be used to cut (destroy) grass if driven recklessly. Crashing into a lawnmower is not encouraged due to the following reasons:

a) it would be very stupid

b) it will screw up your car

c) the lawnmower could be sent tumbling while wielding a spinning blade of destruction.

If you still need additional justification, hitting a lawnmower will make you look fat. Don't do it.

REPEAT (3x):
I WILL NOT CRASH INTO LAWN MOWERS

WATER FALLS

Many people love staring in awe at the sheer power and majesty of a thundering waterfall. You probably just see FREE CAR WASH!

Sure millions of gallons of plummeting water might do a good job at cleaning off all that residue from the fruit stand you decimated, but it is equally likely to destroy your car and leave you 50-100% drowned.

Just wait for it to rain like everybody else does.

REPEAT (3x):
I WILL NOT CRASH INTO WATER FALLS

CONCLUSION

We hope that this guide has been useful and will serve as a valuable reference for you as you embark on your new driving career.

Please refer back to this guide monthly, daily or hourly as necessary to keep up to date on which items are NOT recommended to crash into. If this material is confusing or difficult for you, always remember that other forms of transportation are available. Dog sleds are fashionable, and who wouldn't look great arriving at the club on goat back?

We wish everyone the best of luck.

Drive safe and have fun.

41

Made in the USA
Monee, IL
15 February 2020